The New Kid in Bali

by Eve Beck
illustrated by Nicole Wong

Scott Foresman
is an imprint of

PEARSON

Glenview, Illinois • Boston, Massachusetts • Chandler, Arizona
Upper Saddle River, New Jersey

Every effort has been made to secure permission and provide appropriate credit for photographic material. The publisher deeply regrets any omission and pledges to correct errors called to its attention in subsequent editions.

Unless otherwise acknowledged, all photographs are the property of Scott Foresman, a division of Pearson Education.

Photo locators denoted as follows: Top (T), Center (C), Bottom (B), Left (L), Right (R), Background (Bkgd)

12 ©Adrian Arbib/CORBIS

ISBN 13: 978-0-328-50805-1
ISBN 10:   0-328-50805-5

5 6 7 8 9 10 V010 13 12

My name is Denny. My dad helps out small farms. This summer we went to the country of Bali. That is an island in the Indian Ocean. Kids don't speak English there. They speak Indonesian. But we all know soccer.

My new friend Ketut taught me to say *makanan.* It means "food." Mom and Dad didn't learn any Indonesian words at first. I helped them out a lot.

The food there was good. We ate fried rice, chicken, and ice cream. And you can eat with your fingers. Everyone in Indonesia does that, except Mom and Dad.

In Bali our house was called a *rumah*.
The front door was a gate in a big wall.
We had a beautiful garden to play in.

In a *rumah* all the rooms stand alone. The kitchen is one building. The bathroom is another building. The living room has no walls. My bedroom was like my own little house. At first it was scary. But I started to like it.

In Bali, you go to a temple, not a church. Families drive motorcycles, not cars. Ketut's family took us to a temple.

There was a puppet show at the temple. It lasted all night long. I fell asleep. It was still the best night of our Bali summer.

Now I am back in California. I am in second grade. I fit in here. I dress like my friends. I eat with a knife and fork. The bathroom is down the hall.

But now I miss being the new kid.

I remember Bali. I was the new kid there. It was somewhere that I was someone special. That makes me feel good.

Farms Around the World

Read Together

In this story, you read that Denny's dad helped farmers in Bali. Did you know that there are farming communities all around the world? A farm is a place that grows plants or raises animals for food. In Indonesia, many farms grow rice crops. In the United States, many farms grow wheat crops. In Kenya, some farms raise goats for their milk.

Goat farm in Kenya